WHAT MY EYES SEE THE SCIENCE OF LIGHT

The Science of Light
Children's Physics Books

Speedy Publishing LLC
40 E. Main St. #1156
Newark, DE 19711
www.speedypublishing.com
Copyright 2017

All Rights reserved. No part of this book may be reproduced or used in any way or form or by any means whether electronic or mechanical, this means that you cannot record or photocopy any material ideas or tips that are provided in this book

Have you ever wondered about how your eyes work? What exactly is sight? In this book, you will learn about our amazing eyes, how we are able to see what we see, as well as how they interact with light.

EYES AND SIGHT

We are lucky to enjoy sight as one of our five senses to assist in obtaining information about what is happening around us. We have the ability to see with our eyes, the organs that take in the light and images and create electrical impulses for our brain to absorb and understand.

HOW DO WE SEE?

Reflected light is actually what we see when we see something. Its rays reflect from objects into our eyes.

OUR EYEBALLS ARE AMAZING

Listed below are the parts of the eyes.

PUPIL AND IRIS:

Our eyes are complex and amazing organs. For us to be able to see, the light enters into our eyes through that black spot which is located in the middle of the eye, which actually is a hole and it is referred to as the pupil.

It changes size with assistance of the area around it called the iris, which is a color such as blue, brown, green or hazel.

    The iris is actually a muscle. The iris controls the amount of light that gets into the eye by closing and opening the pupil. The pupil is able to control the amount of light that gets into the eye if it is too bright by shrinking to let less in, therefore protecting the eye.

RETINA:

Once light gets to our eye, it goes through fluids and ends up on the retina located at the rear of our eye. The retina is then able to turn its rays of light into signals for our brain to understand.

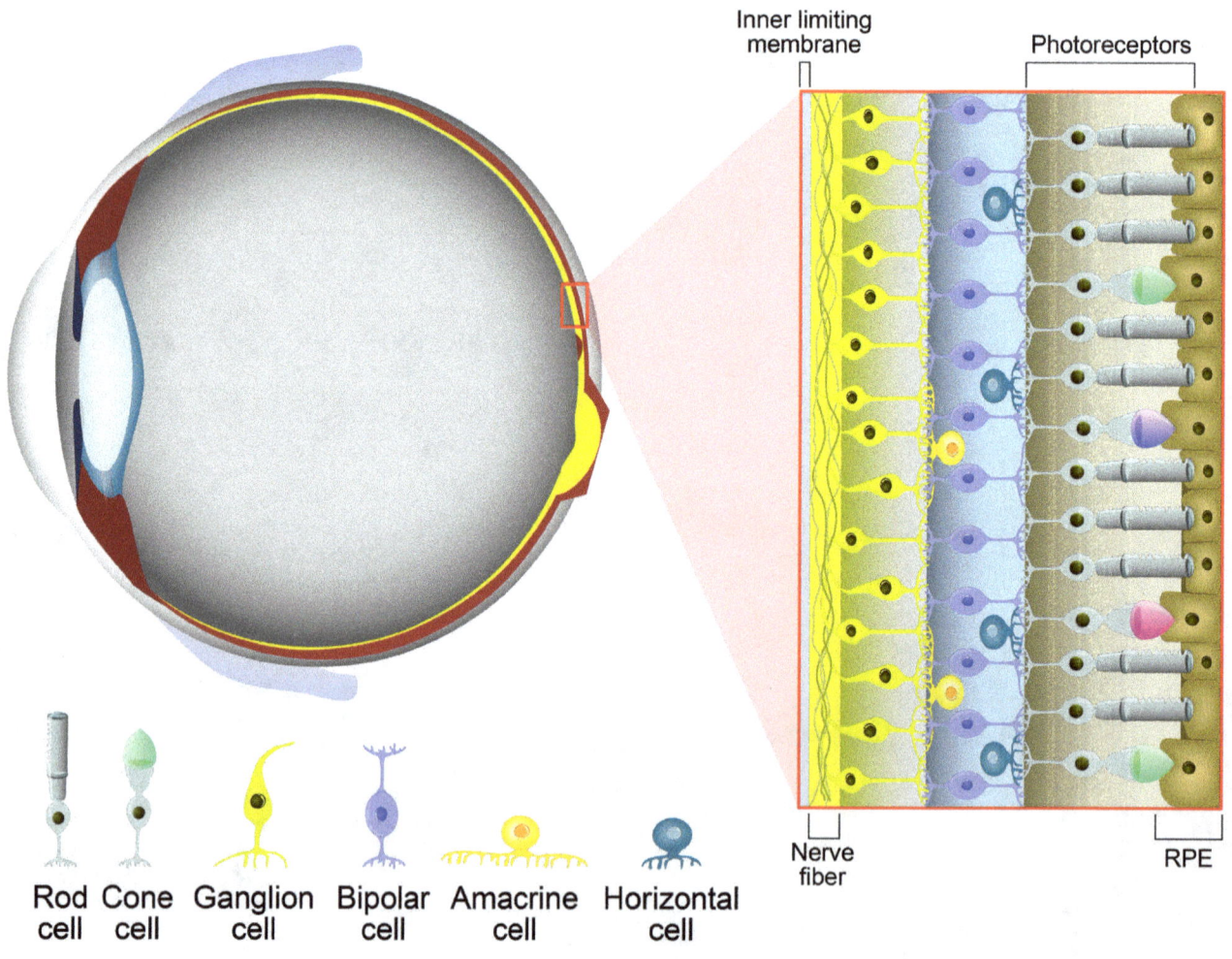

It uses rods, which are light sensitive cells, and cones to see. The rods help us see when it's dark as they are extremely sensitive to light. We are able to see color because of the cones. There are three different kinds of cones, with each one of them helping us to see different colors of light: blue, green and red.

When an image gets to the retina, it is seen as upside down from the actual image. It is up to our brain to switch it around for us so that we can see it as it is supposed to be seen.

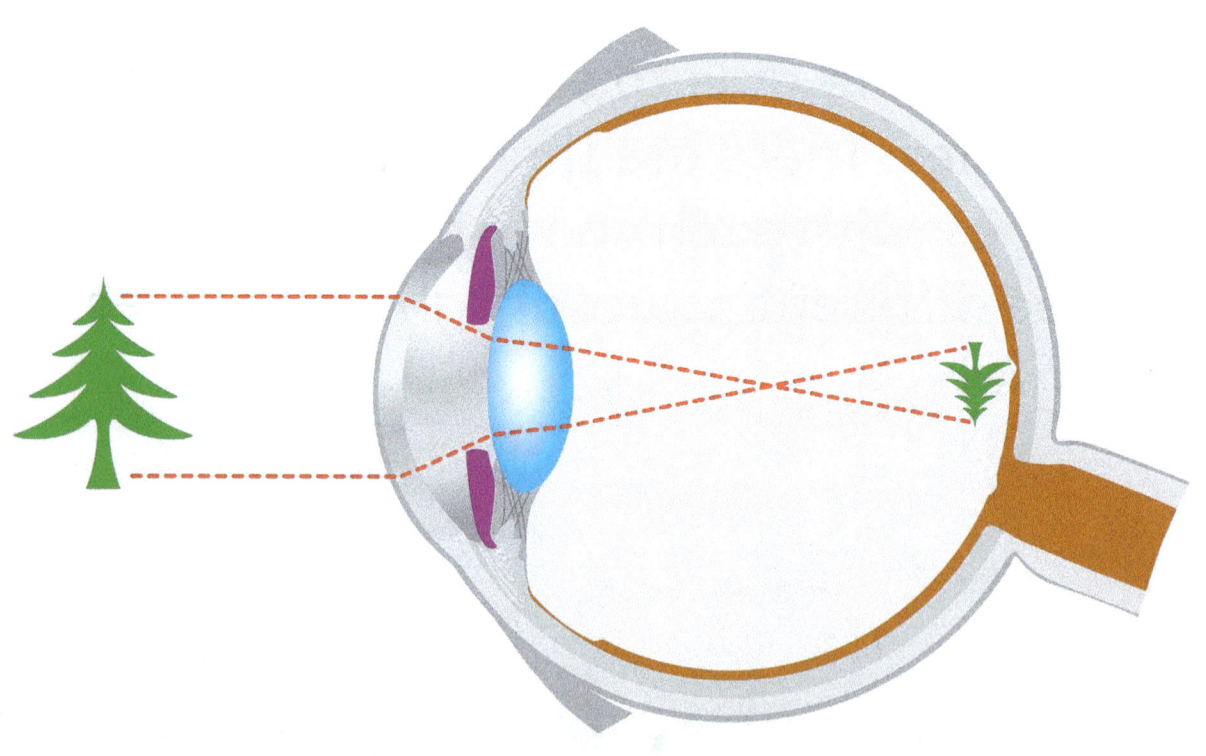

FOCUS:

For light to be focused on our retina, we have a lens in our eyes. The brain sends signals to the muscles surrounding the lens telling it how to focus the light.

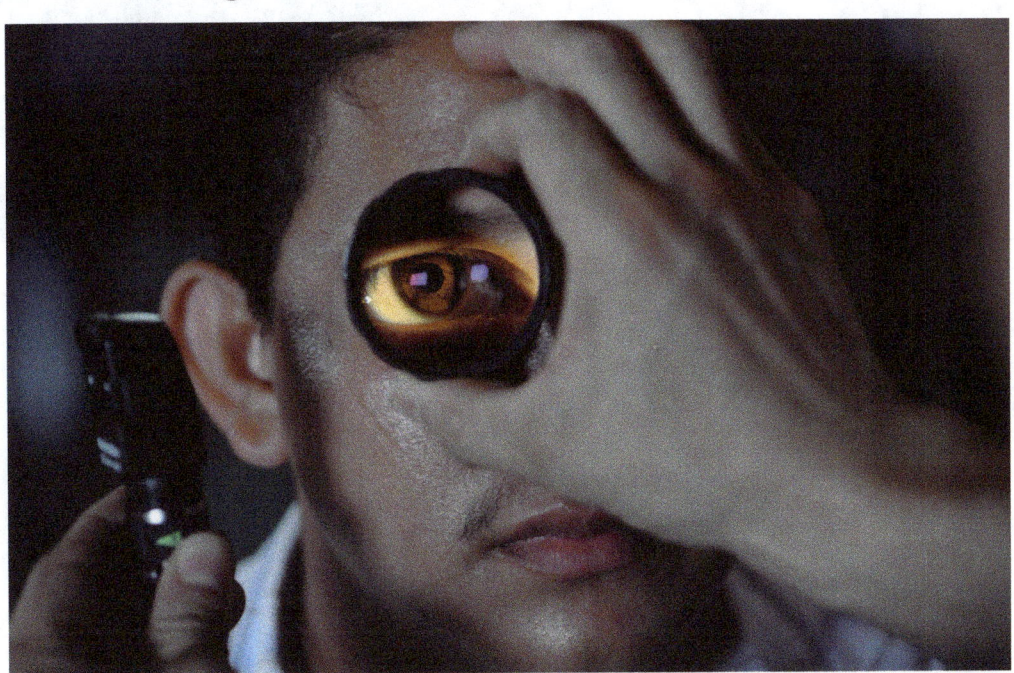

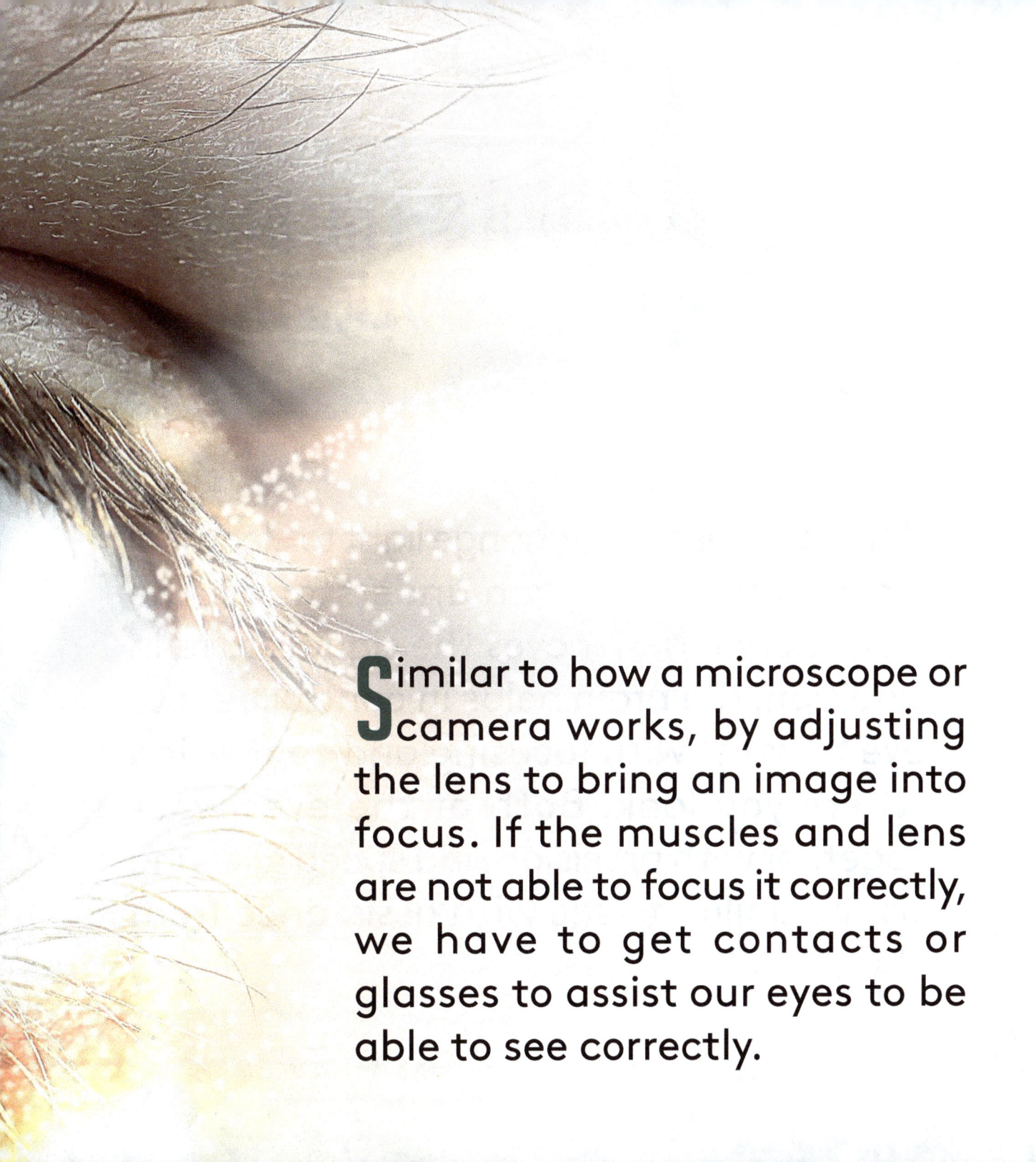

Similar to how a microscope or camera works, by adjusting the lens to bring an image into focus. If the muscles and lens are not able to focus it correctly, we have to get contacts or glasses to assist our eyes to be able to see correctly.

HOW DOES THE BRAIN UNDERSTAND?

The cones and rods change light to electrical signal that our brain understands. The optic nerve then moves the signals to it. In addition, the brain helps in controlling our eye to assist with focusing and controlling where you look. Both of the eyes work together with precision and speed allowing us the ability to see with assistance from the brain.

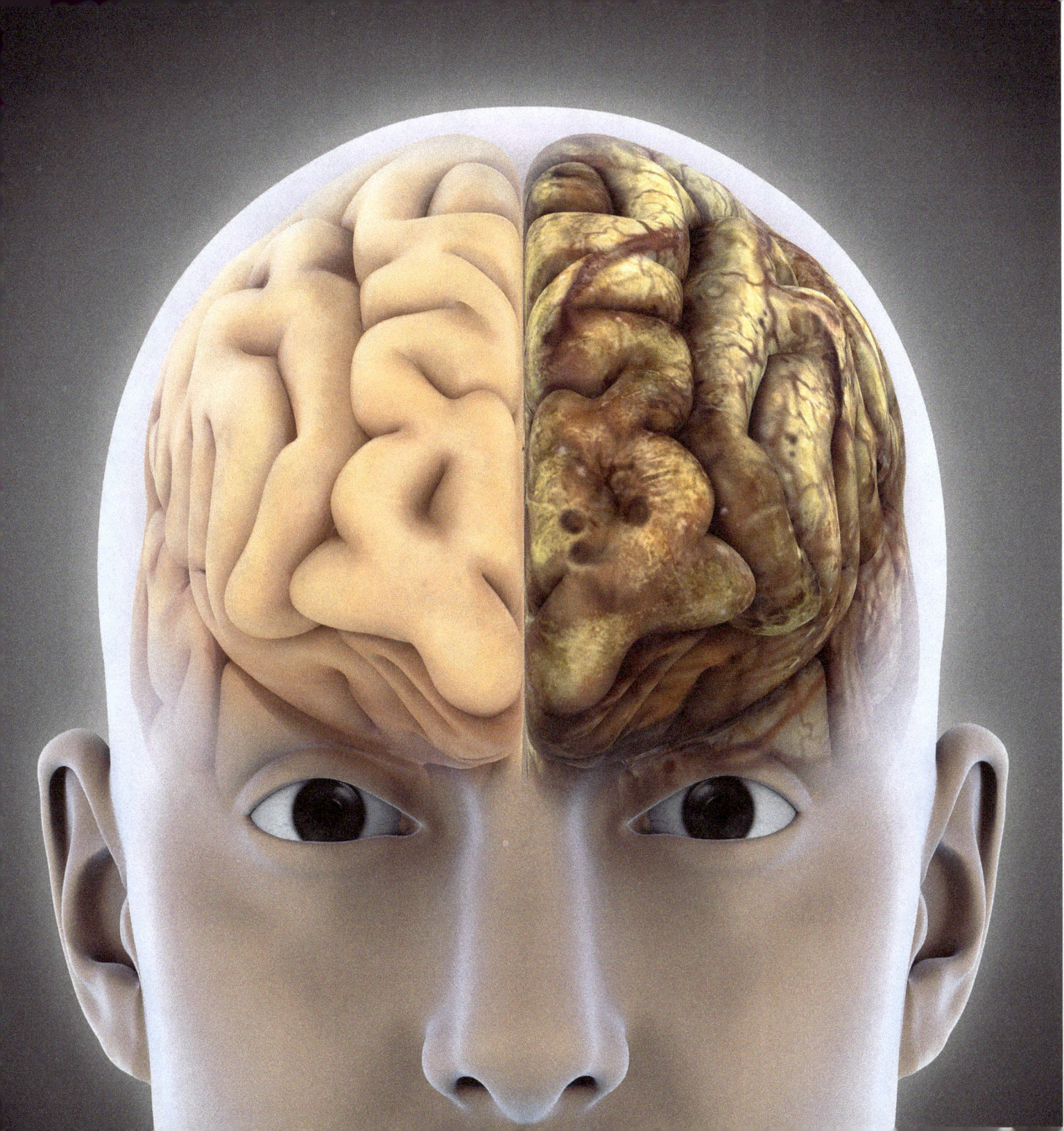

WHY DO WE HAVE TWO EYEBALLS?

Having two eyeballs lets our brain receive two somewhat pictures at different angles. While we only see one image, the brain needs the two images to provide us with information as to how far away something is located. This is referred to as depth perception.

WHAT IS COLOR BLINDNESS?

A friend might tease you that if your clothes don't match you must be color blind. But, there are cases of people that actually are color blind.

While it may not mean that they cannot see any colors at all, it does mean that they have difficulty seeing different colors. It's not like seeing a black and white movie.

It actually can make it difficult to match your pants to your shirt, but it is not a serious issue. People that are color blind are able to do normal everyday stuff, including driving. While most people that are color-blind cannot distinguish between green or red, they are able to learn to respond to how traffic signals are set up – such as that the red light typically is on the top and the green light is typically on the bottom.

In order to understand how color blindness occurs, you have to learn about the cones that are in your eyes. These cones are very small and are cells on the retina of the eye, an area approximately the size of postage stamp located near the back of your eye.

As discussed earlier, there are green, blue and red cones, and they are sensitive to each of those colors as well as combinations of the three colors.

Photoreceptor cell

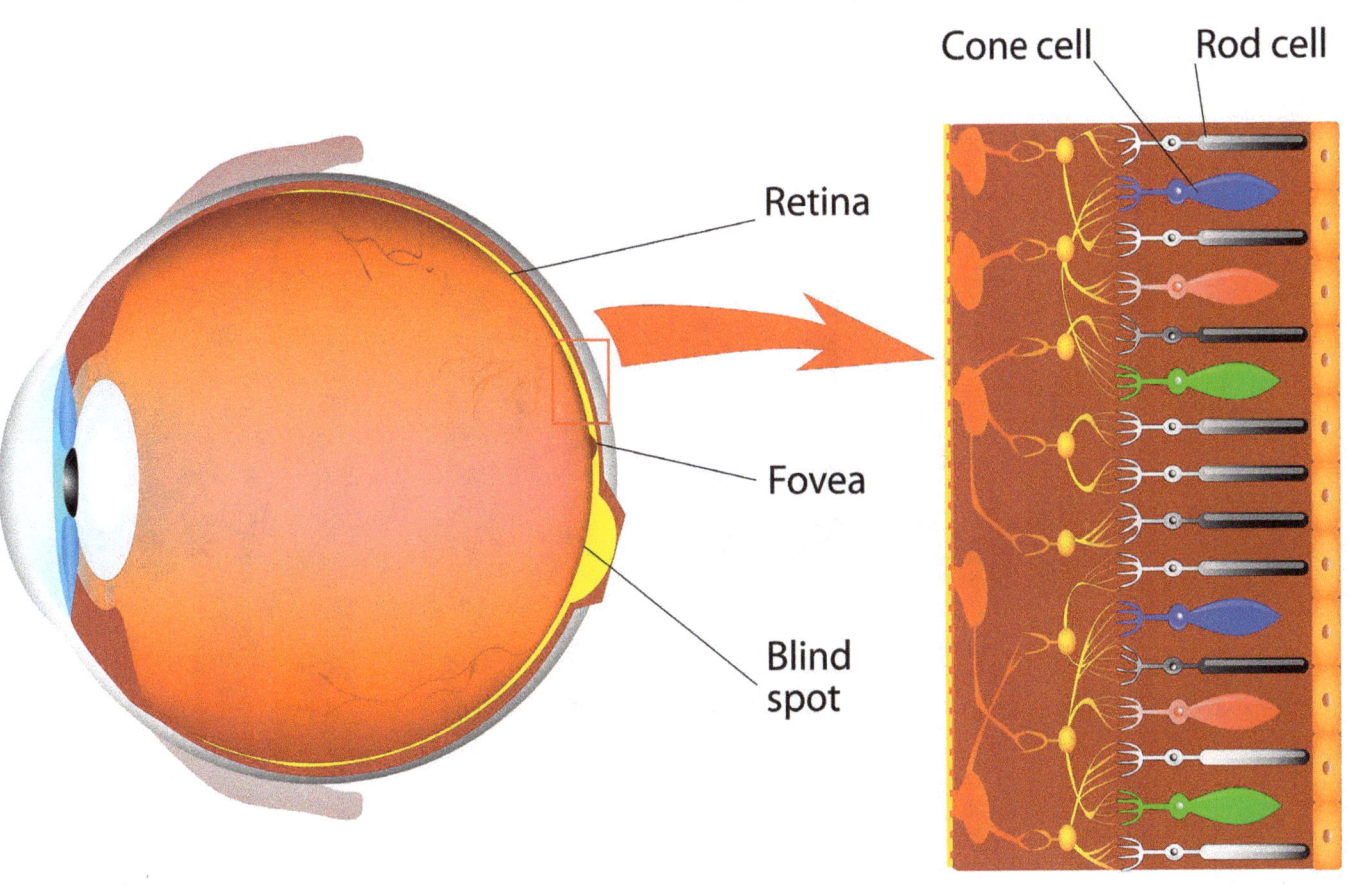

If the cones are not working correctly, or they are not working in the correct combination, you brain will not receive the correct message

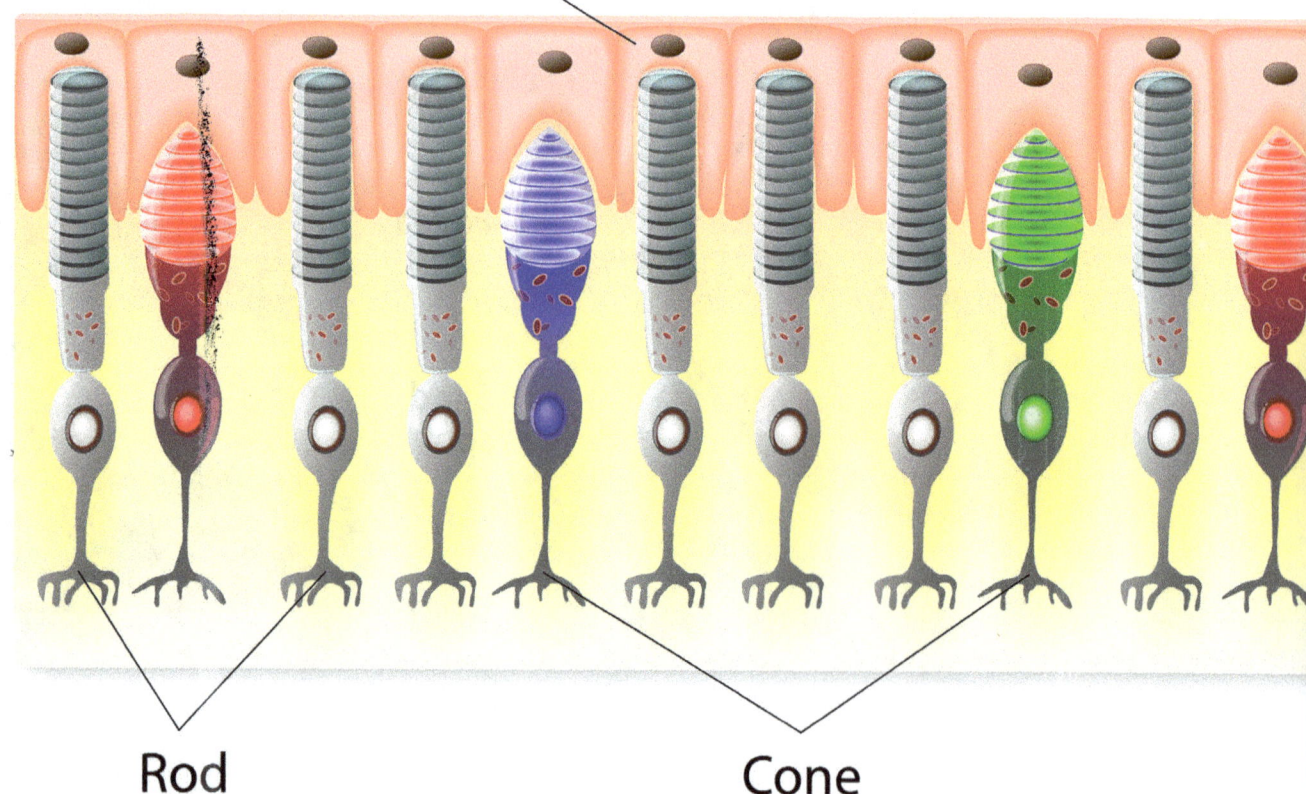

Pigment epithelium

Rod

Cone

about what colors you are actually seeing. For someone that is color blind, a leaf that is green may appear as gray or tan.

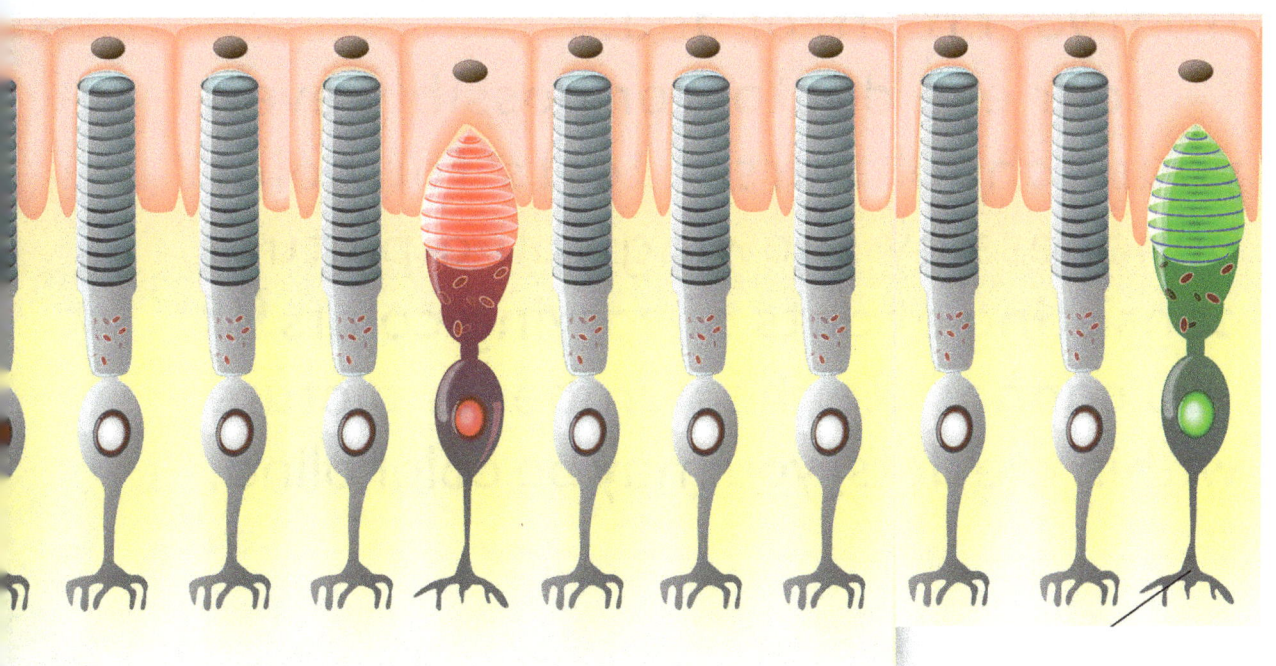

Color blindness is pretty much always inherited, meaning that you get it from your mom or dad.

Your eye doctor, or possibly even your school nurse, tests for color blindness by showing you a picture consisting of dots of varying colors. If you cannot see the number or picture within the dots, you may be color blind.

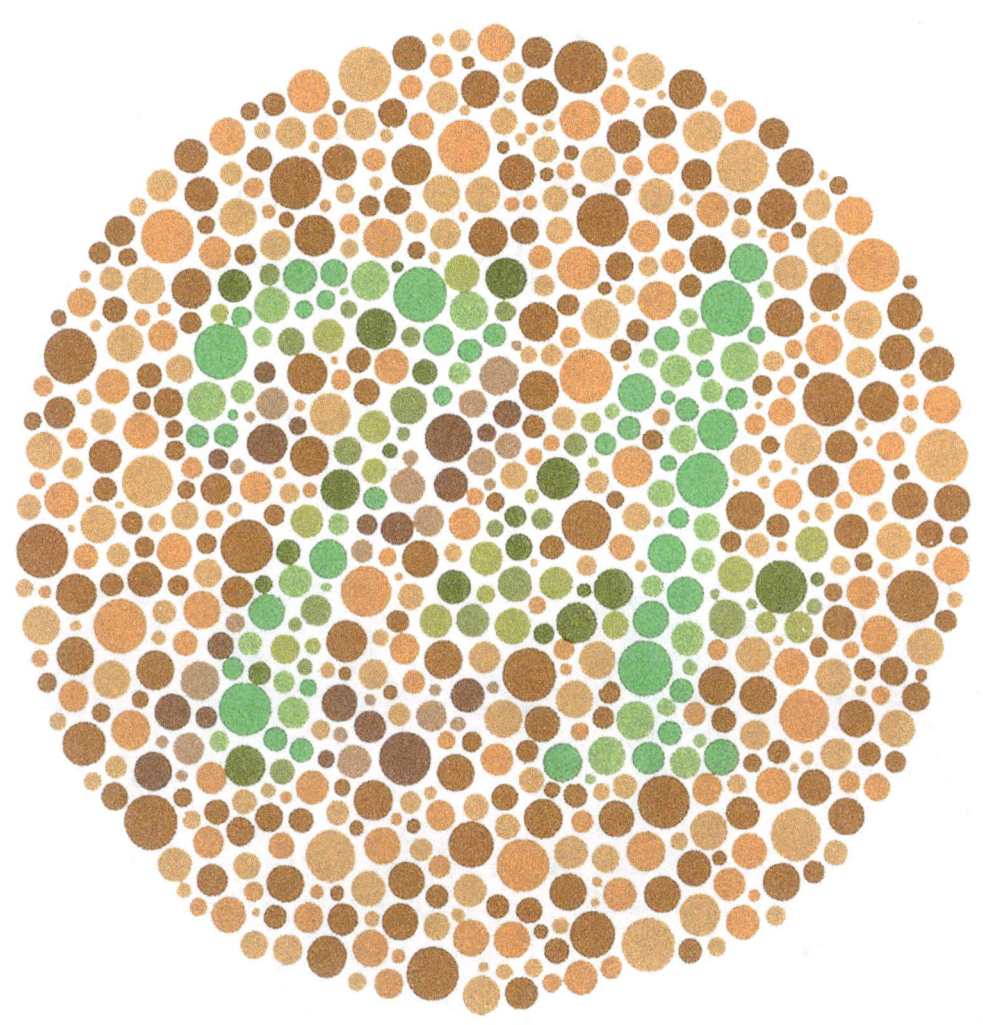

A COLOR BLIND TEST

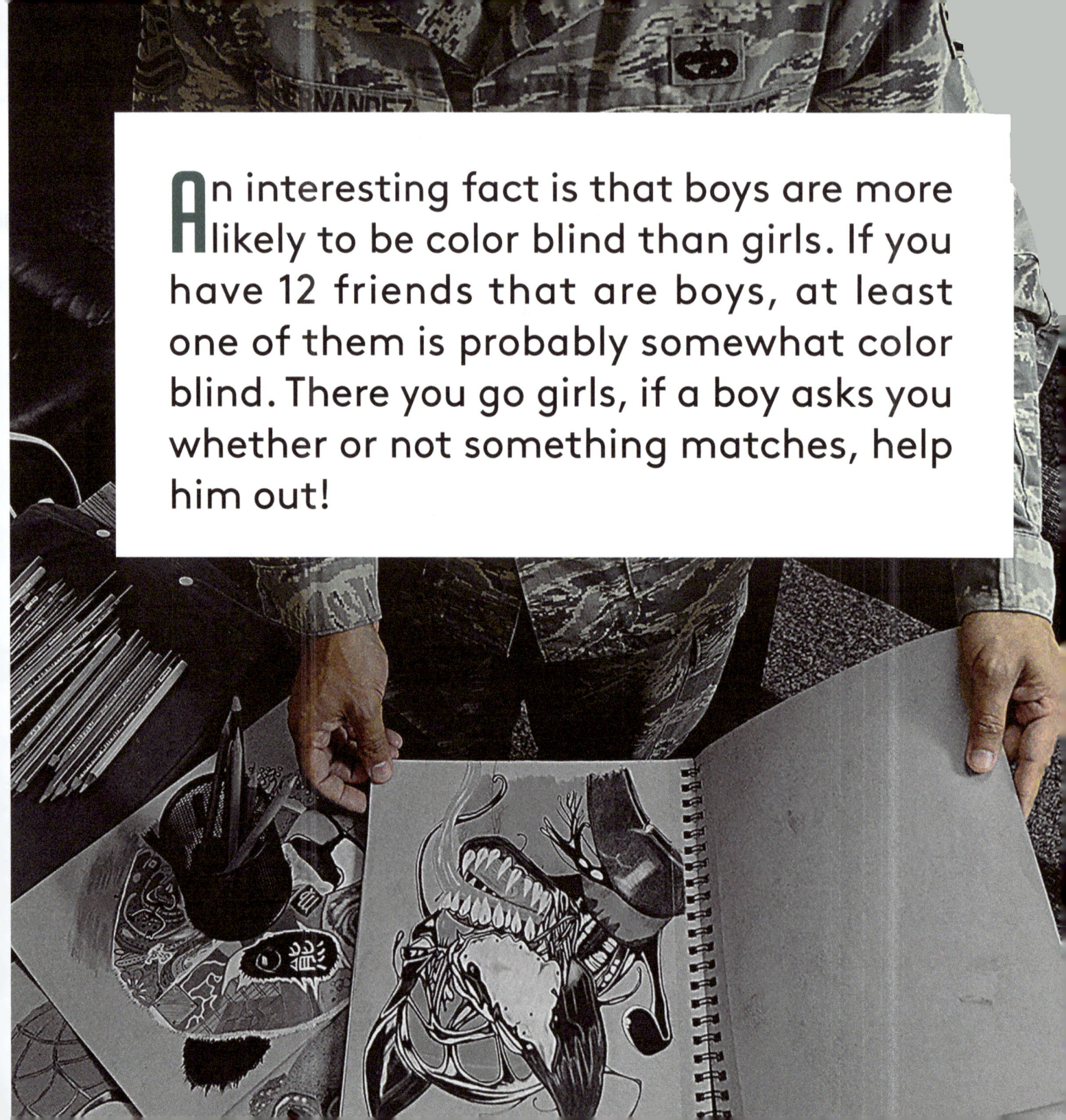

An interesting fact is that boys are more likely to be color blind than girls. If you have 12 friends that are boys, at least one of them is probably somewhat color blind. There you go girls, if a boy asks you whether or not something matches, help him out!

THE SCIENCE OF LIGHT

20/70	T O Z	70 FT. 21.3 m	3
20/50	L P E D	50 FT. 15.2 m	4
20/40	P E C F D	40 FT. 12.2 m	5
20/30	E D F C Z P	30 FT. 9.14 m	6

WHAT IS IT MADE OF?

Light is not really considered to be matter, and it has no mass. Scientists today believe it is an energy form consisting of photons. It is unique since it behaves like a wave and a particle.

WHY DOES IT GO THROUGH THIS AND NOT THAT?

Light behaves differently dependent upon the type of matter that it contacts. Occasionally it will pass right through the matter, such as water or air. This is known as transparent matter.

THE CURTAIN OF THIS ROOM IS TRANSLUCENT.

Other items will totally reflect it, such as a book or an animal. These are referred to as opaque objects. There is also a third type of object that does a bit of both and might scatter the light. These are known as translucent objects.

LIGHT HELPS US SURVIVE THE WORLD WE LIVE IN

If we did not have sunlight, we would be in a dark, dead place. In addition to helping us to see, sunlight also keeps our planet warm, so that it is now frozen in outer space. It also plays a major role in photosynthesis, which is how plants grow and get the nutrients they need. It also is a great source of energy and provides vitamin D that we need.

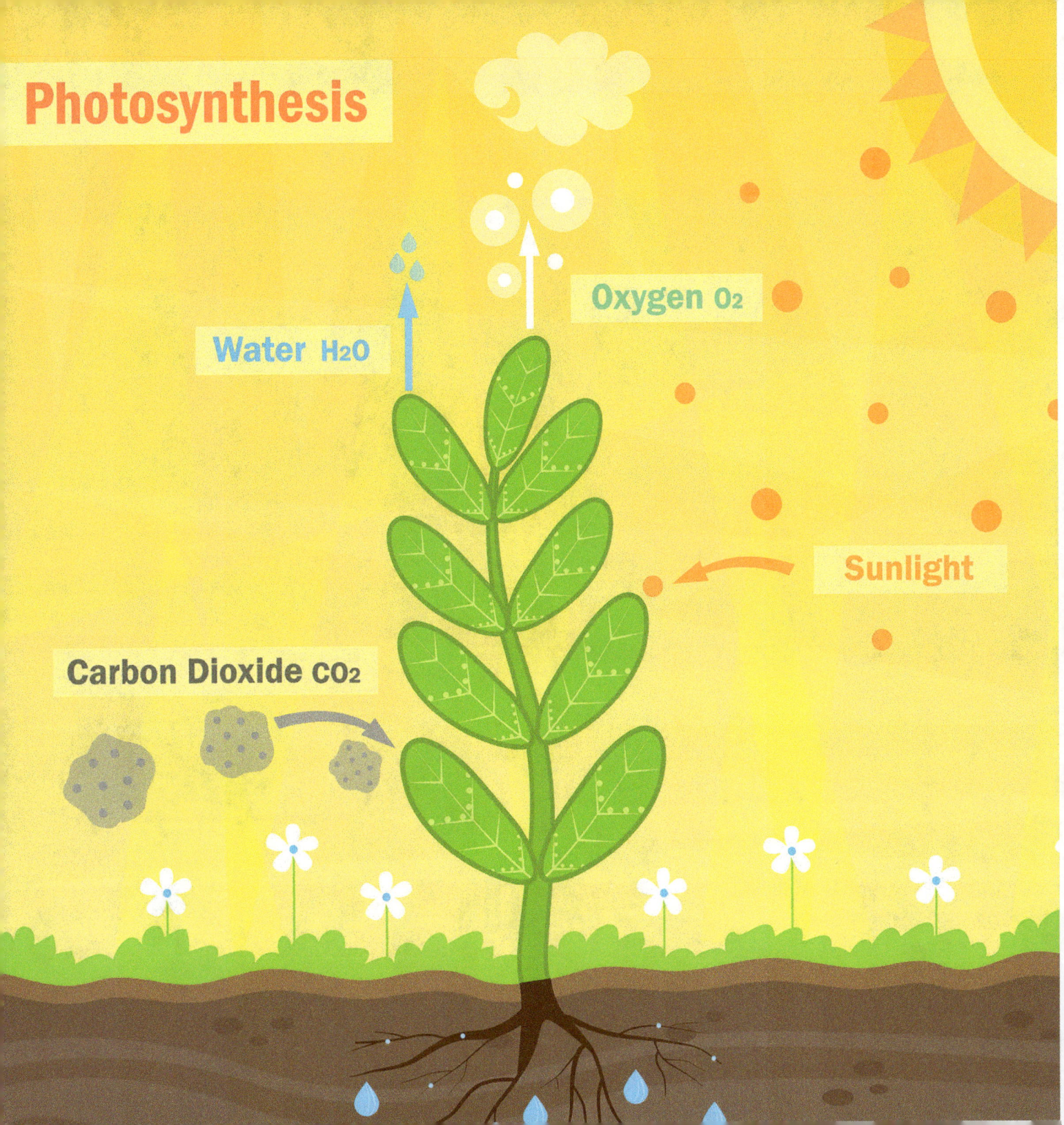

HOW FAST CAN LIGHT TRAVEL?

Light is the quickest moving speed of the universe. There is nothing that is able to move faster, or get even close to, the speed of light. When it is in a vacuum, with nothing slowing it down, it travels at 186,282 miles per second. That is pretty amazing! It might be slowed down a bit when it travels through air or water, but it is still amazingly quick.

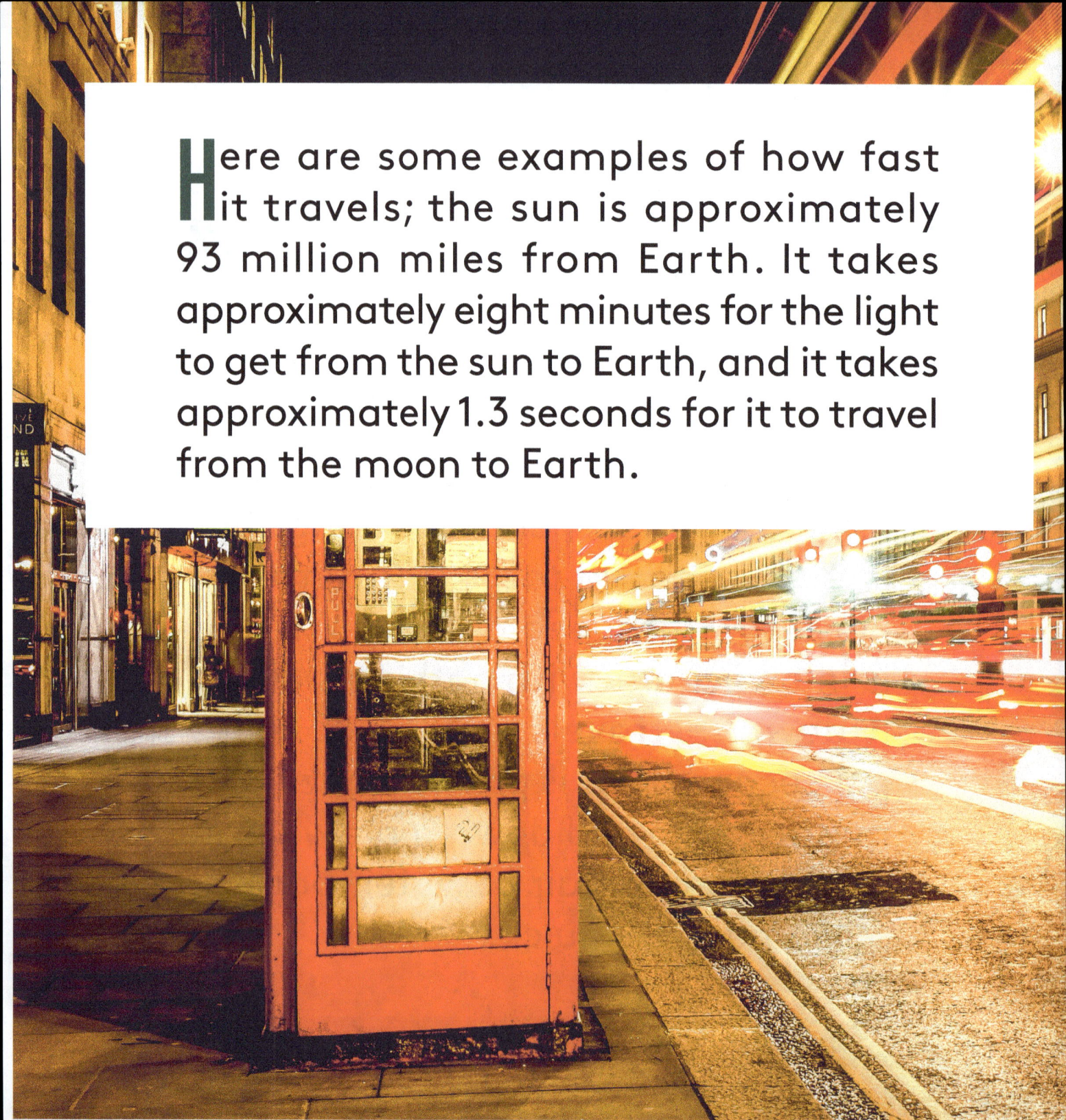

Here are some examples of how fast it travels; the sun is approximately 93 million miles from Earth. It takes approximately eight minutes for the light to get from the sun to Earth, and it takes approximately 1.3 seconds for it to travel from the moon to Earth.

REFRACTION

Typically, light will travel a straight path referred to as a ray, but when it passes through a transparent object such as glass or water, it turns or bends. This is the result of different mediums or materials having different structures.

In every medium type, whether it is water or air or glass, the light's wavelength will be altered, but its frequency will not be altered. This results in the speed and direction of the moving wave of light changing and it appears to change directions or bend.

A prism is a great example of a refraction. Prisms are unique since each light color is refracted at a different angle. It has the ability to take the white light from the sun and then proceed to send out various colors of light, which can be beautiful.

Our lenses use refraction in helping us to see things. Microscopes help us to see very tiny things while telescopes enable us to see things that are far away. If you wear glasses, they also use refraction to help us see everyday items better.

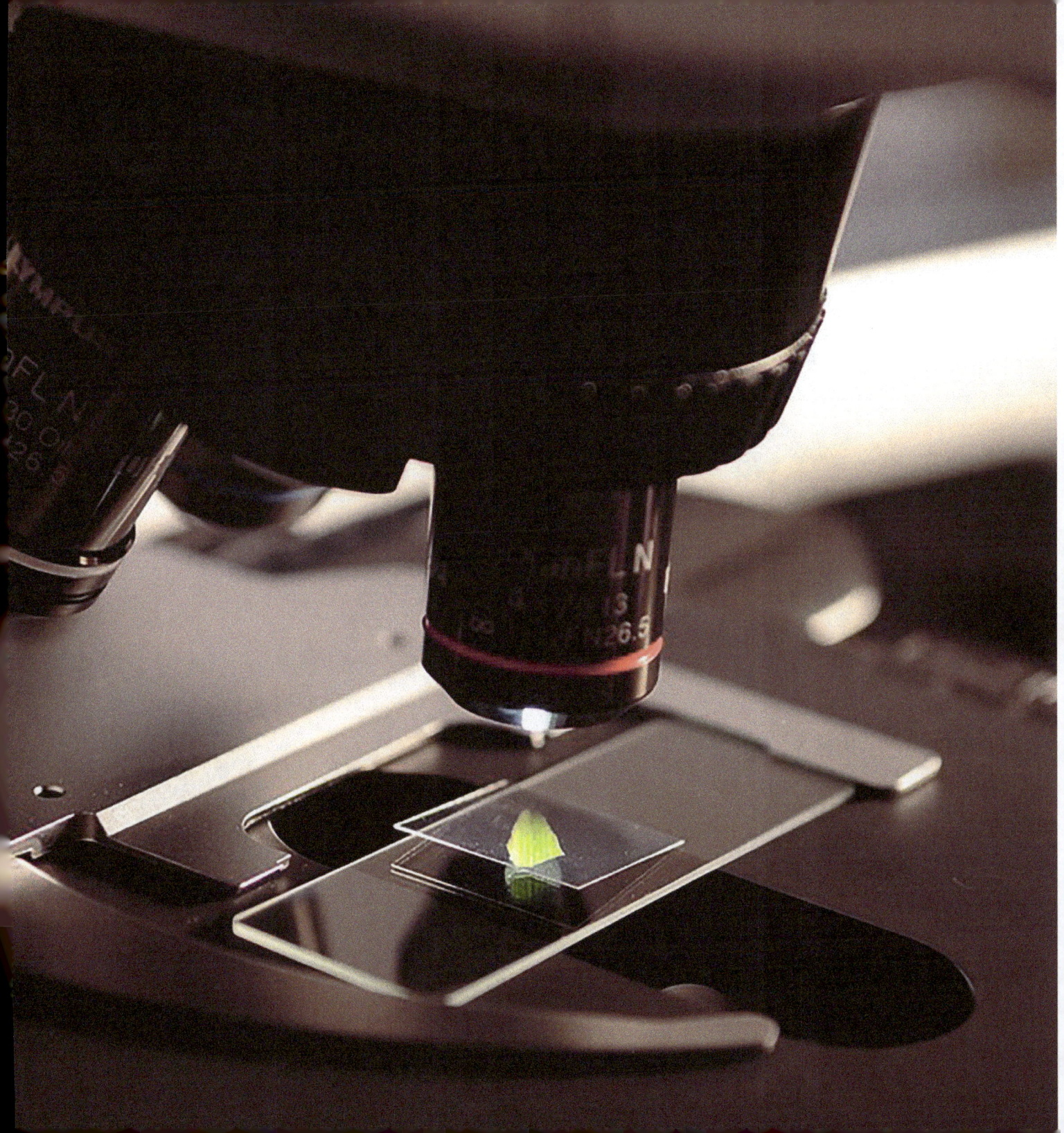

Isn't it amazing how everything works together so that we can see? Think about it the next time you see the sun and how fast that light travels so that we can enjoy it.

For additional information about your eyes, light, and how it all works together you can go to your local library, research the internet, or ask questions of your teachers, family, and friends.

CPSIA information can be obtained
at www.ICGtesting.com
Printed in the USA
BVHW011303160921
616897BV00015B/147